STARTUP
TO
SCALE-UP

Unlocking Growth with Smart Funding

A Practical Funding Guide for Business Owners and Professionals

CA KRISHN KUMAR BAHETI

About the Author

 **Krishn Kumar Baheti** is a seasoned Chartered Accountant and the founder of Baheti Financial Services and K K Baheti & Co., which specializes in comprehensive funding solutions, financial advisory, and a wide range of Chartered Accountancy services across India. With over ten years of experience, he has helped businesses of all sizes unlock growth opportunities.

Krishn's expertise spans secured and unsecured financing, CGTMSE schemes, business loan portfolio management, lease rental discounting (LRD), private funding, overdraft (OD) and cash credit (CC) facilities, invoice discounting, machinery loans, working capital loans, project financing, equity financing, SME IPO preparation, various government schemes, and credit repair. He also specializes in startup funding, providing tailored strategies to help new ventures scale operations through smart funding solutions.

Beyond funding, K K Baheti & Co. offers a full suite of Chartered Accountancy services, including taxation advisory, audit and assurance, GST compliance, corporate structuring, business valuation, and regulatory compliance. Krishn's multidisciplinary expertise allows him to deliver integrated solutions to MSMEs, startups, and established enterprises.

In addition to being a Chartered Accountant, Krishn holds prestigious qualifications including a Diploma in IFRS from ACCA (UK), and certifications in Fundamental Analysis on Equity and Derivatives (FATA), and Foreign Exchange and Treasury Management. His holistic approach combines technical knowledge with practical insights, empowering MSMEs, startups, and established businesses to navigate complex financial landscapes.

Through his books—'Startup to Scale-Up: Unlock Growth with Smart Funding' and others—Krishn empowers MSMEs, chartered accountants, and entrepreneurs with actionable insights to navigate financial complexities and scale their businesses through various funding options. In addition to his advisory work, he shares his expertise through webinars, publications, and Instagram & YouTube channel dedicated to financial literacy and funding strategies. He actively engages with his audience on Instagram, X (formerly Twitter), and LinkedIn, where he provides valuable insights on business funding, compliance, and financial growth.

ABOUT THE BOOK

Aman, an ambitious entrepreneur, dreams of scaling his startup but feels lost in the complex funding world. Ankit, a Chartered accountant and a seasoned funding expert, becomes his mentor, guiding him through bootstrapping, bank loans, venture capital, and government schemes. Through their engaging conversations, Aman discovers the step-by-step process to identify funding needs, prepare effective pitches, and negotiate with investors while retaining control of his business.

As their dialogue unfolds, Aman learns not just about the different funding sources but also how to evaluate which option aligns with his business goals. From understanding the nuances of term sheets to leveraging government grants and schemes, Ankit offers actionable insights drawn from years of real-world experience. Each chapter of this book reflects the challenges many entrepreneurs face and provides clear frameworks to overcome them.

Whether you're bootstrapping a new venture or managing an established business, this book equips you with the knowledge to secure the right capital at the right time. Through Aman's journey, you'll discover practical tools to craft a compelling pitch, understand investor expectations, and negotiate terms without losing sight of your long-term vision.

This guide is designed for entrepreneurs who want to scale their businesses, business owners seeking to diversify funding sources, and professionals advising clients on financial growth. Each concept is explained in a simple, conversational style to make complex funding strategies accessible and actionable.

By the end of this book, you'll have the tools to:

- Identify and evaluate different funding sources.

- Prepare compelling business pitches and financial documents.

- Navigate the negotiation process with confidence.

- Utilize government schemes and grants effectively.

- Manage post-funding growth while maintaining control of your business.

Aman's journey mirrors the path many entrepreneurs take—full of ambition, challenges, and the need for the right guidance. Ankit's expertise provides a clear roadmap to unlock funding and fuel business growth. This book is not just about securing capital; it's about empowering you to take your startup to scale-up with clarity and confidence.

Who This Book Is For

Ask yourself these questions:

- Are you an entrepreneur struggling to find the right funding to grow your business?

- Are you a startup founder unsure about navigating bank loans, venture capital, or government grants?

- Are you a business owner looking to expand operations without losing control?

- Are you a chartered accountant or financial professional wanting to provide better funding advice to your clients?

- Are you a consultant or advisor seeking deeper insights into modern funding strategies and financial instruments?

- Are you an aspiring entrepreneur looking to understand the funding landscape before you launch?

If you answered **YES** to any of these questions, then **this book is for you**. Whether you are just starting or aiming to scale your business, this book will empower you with the knowledge and tools to secure capital, unlock growth, and succeed in today's competitive market.

ACKNOWLEDGEMENT

I extend my heartfelt gratitude to everyone who contributed to the creation of this book. Special thanks to my colleagues, mentors, and clients whose insights and experiences have enriched the content.

I am especially thankful to the chartered accountants, business owners, and entrepreneurs who shared their real-life challenges and triumphs. Their openness provided invaluable lessons and practical insights that shaped these pages.

I am deeply grateful to my family—my parents, sister, and wife—for their unwavering support and patience throughout this journey. Your encouragement has been a constant source of strength. To my friends and peers, your feedback and thought-provoking discussions have sharpened the ideas presented here.

A special note of appreciation goes to my mentor, whose guidance and wisdom have been invaluable. Your insights have helped shape this work into a practical and effective resource.

Lastly, thank you, the reader, for trusting this book. It empowers you to make informed decisions, unlock new opportunities, and achieve sustainable business growth.

Disclaimer

The information in this book is for general guidance only and does not constitute professional financial, legal, or tax advice. Although every effort has been made to ensure accuracy, laws and regulations may change, and individual circumstances vary.

Readers should consult qualified professionals before making any financial or business decisions. The author and publisher disclaim any liability for actions taken based on this content.

Examples and case studies are illustrative and may not apply to every situation. Any resemblance to real persons, businesses, or events is purely coincidental unless explicitly stated. All characters, entities, and scenarios depicted in this book are purely fictional and are used solely for educational and illustrative purposes.

By using this book, you accept full responsibility for your decisions and agree that the author and publisher are not liable for any outcomes resulting from the information provided.

Table of Contents

Chapter 1

Mapping Your Path from Startup to Scale-Up

Aman leaned back in his chair, sipping on his third cup of coffee. It was late, but his mind buzzed with questions about his growing business. After months of hard work, he had paying customers and increasing demand. Yet, as revenue grew, so did the expenses.

His phone buzzed. It was Ankit, his childhood friend and a Chartered Accountant, who had helped countless businesses navigate their financial journeys. Aman smiled. If anyone could help him figure out the next steps, it would be Ankit.

"Hey Aman, what's up? Still burning the midnight oil?" Ankit's voice was warm but sharp.

"Always," Aman chuckled. "But listen, I need your help. We're growing faster than I expected, and I'm already struggling to keep up with working capital. Should I be looking for funding now, or is it too early?"

Ankit laughed softly. "It's never too early to think about funding—but first, let's figure out exactly what you need. Tell me, where do things stand right now?"

1.1 Understanding the Business Lifecycle: Startup, Growth, and Scale-Up

"Well," Aman began, "we started with a simple idea and bootstrapped everything through personal savings and a little help from family. Now, things are moving quickly, and I'm struggling to manage the financial side."

"Sounds like you're moving from the Startup Stage to the Growth Stage," Ankit said. "At this point, cash flow issues are common—you're spending faster to keep up with demand. The question is: do you need money for operations or expansion?"

Aman frowned. "Honestly? Both. I need to hire more people, invest in better systems, and manage the day-to-day bills."

"Classic growth-stage problems," Ankit said. "Let me break it down for you."

Startup Stage: Where You Began

"In the startup stage, you focused on building your product or service and proving your idea. Funding here usually comes from personal savings, family, and small grants," Ankit explained.

"Yeah, I know that pain," Aman laughed. "Every rupee mattered."

"Exactly. At this stage, investors care about whether you can solve a real problem and whether customers will pay for it."

Growth Stage: Where You Are Now

"You've proven your idea works," Ankit continued. "Now, in the growth stage, the goal is to scale operations—hire staff, invest in technology, and reach more customers. This is where you start looking at funding like working capital loans, OD/CC, and even venture capital if you want to grow fast."

"So, I need more than just a quick cash fix," Aman mused.

"Right. You're building the machine now—you want to fuel it properly, not just patch leaks."

Scale-Up Stage: Where You Want to Go

"And after that comes the scale-up stage, where businesses expand into new markets and raise larger capital through private equity, IPOs, or strategic partnerships," Ankit explained.

"Whoa, slow down," Aman laughed. "I'm still trying to survive month-to-month!"

"Fair," Ankit smiled. "But understanding the full journey helps you decide your next move. So—let's focus on where you are now."

1.2 Why Funding is Essential for Each Stage

"So, you're saying I definitely need funding—but why can't I just grow slowly and fund it through my profits?" Aman asked.

"You could," Ankit admitted, "but here's the catch—without funding, you're limiting your growth potential. Imagine if a competitor with deeper pockets swoops in while you're struggling to deliver your orders."

"That's a scary thought," Aman murmured.

"It should be," Ankit said. "With the right funding, you can:

Invest in Growth: Scale operations and stay ahead of the competition.

Enhance Market Competitiveness: Capture a larger market share quickly.

Ensure Business Continuity: Handle sudden expenses or slow payment cycles without breaking a sweat."

Aman sighed. "Alright, I'm convinced. But how do I know how much funding I actually need?"

1.3 Identifying Your Business's Funding Needs

"Great question," Ankit said. "Let's break it down."

Step 1: Analyze Business Objectives

"First, be clear on why you need funding. Are you trying to manage working capital, invest in technology, or expand your team?"

Aman nodded. "All three, honestly. But I guess working capital is the most urgent."

Step 2: Evaluate Your Current Financial Health

"How's your cash flow?" Ankit asked.

"Tight," Aman admitted. "I have enough to cover next month's expenses, but if we grow faster, I'm in trouble."

"Good to know," Ankit said. "Lenders and investors will want to see your financial statements—profit and loss, cash flow forecasts, and even your credit history."

Step 3: Determine Funding Type & Amount

"Lastly, figure out how much you need and the best type of funding," Ankit continued.

"Debt or equity?" Aman asked.

"For now, probably debt—like a working capital loan or an OD/CC facility," Ankit suggested. "It's cheaper, and you keep full control of your business."

✅ Checklist 1: Business Funding Needs Assessment

"Let's go through a quick checklist to confirm what you need," Ankit said.

Criteria	Yes/No	Details
Have you clearly defined your funding purpose?		

Is your business ready for external funding?		
Have you calculated the exact funding amount?		
Do you understand the risks of different funding types?		
Are you prepared with financial statements and documentation?		
Have you outlined a repayment or return strategy?		

Aman sighed. "Looks like I've got work to do."

In Summary

"So," Ankit said, "you've moved beyond the startup phase, and you're now navigating the growth stage—where funding is crucial to avoid cash flow problems and stay competitive. The key is to assess your exact needs and choose the right funding type without giving up too much control."

"Got it," Aman said, determination in his voice. "What's my next step?"

"Next," Ankit smiled, "we dive into the **funding foundations** and how to unlock the best ones for your business."

Chapter 2

Funding Foundations – Key Concepts You Must Know

The next day, Aman met Ankit at their favorite coffee shop. Armed with his notebook and a million questions, he was ready to explore the world of funding further.

"So, where do we start?" Aman asked, stirring his coffee.

Ankit smiled. "Let's begin with the basics—you need to understand the core concepts of business funding before you can choose the right option."

2.1 Debt vs. Equity: Understanding the Core Difference

Aman leaned forward. "Okay, I get that I need funding—but should I get a loan, or should I give away equity to an investor?"

"Great question," Ankit said. "Let's break it down simply:

Debt: You borrow money, and repay it with interest, but keep 100% control of your business.

Equity involves selling a portion of your business in exchange for funds, which means giving up ownership but without repayment pressure.

Aman nodded slowly. "So, debt means I owe money, but equity means I give up a slice of my business. Which is better?"

"It depends on your situation," Ankit explained. "If you want to keep control and have a stable cash flow for repayments, debt works best. But if you're aiming for rapid growth and can't afford to repay immediately, equity might be a better fit."

When to Choose Debt Funding

- When you need quick capital for working capital or an asset purchase.

- If you want to retain control of your business decisions.

- When your cash flow is stable enough to manage repayments.

Example: A retail business using an overdraft facility (OD) to manage seasonal inventory needs.

When to Choose Equity Funding

- When you want to scale rapidly and need large capital without monthly repayments.

- If you are open to sharing ownership and strategic decisions.

- When you lack collateral for a loan.

Example: A tech startup raising funds from angel investors to expand into new markets.

Aman sighed. "I guess I'm leaning toward debt—I'm not ready to give up control."

"Smart move," Ankit said. "Let's explore more funding options."

2.2 Secured vs. Unsecured Loans: Which One Fits Your Business?

Aman scratched his head. "What's the difference between secured and unsecured loans?"

"Simple," Ankit replied. "A secured loan requires you to pledge collateral—like property, inventory, or receivables—while an unsecured loan doesn't require any collateral but comes with higher interest rates."

Secured Loans

Pros:

- Lower interest rates

- Larger loan amounts are available.

Cons:

- Requires valuable collateral (property, machinery, etc.).

- Risk of losing the asset if you default.

Examples:

- Loan Against Property (LAP)

- Lease Rental Discounting (LRD)

- Working Capital Term Loan

Unsecured Loans

Pros:

- No collateral required.

- Faster approval and disbursement.

Cons:

- Higher interest rates

- Lower loan amounts.

Examples:

- Business Loans from NBFCs

- Overdraft (OD) / Cash Credit (CC)

- Revenue-Based Financing

"So, which one fits your business better?" Ankit asked.

Aman thought for a moment. "I don't have major assets to pledge, so an unsecured loan seems more realistic for me right now."

"Exactly," Ankit said. "But there are more nuances to explore."

2.3 Short-Term vs. Long-Term Funding: Timing Matters

"Okay," Aman said, "I need to grow fast—but how do I decide between short-term and long-term funding?"

"It depends on what you need the money for," Ankit explained.

Short-Term Funding

Duration: Less than 12 months.

Best for: Immediate working capital, managing cash flow gaps.

Examples: OD/CC limits, invoice discounting, bridge loans.

Use Case: You need funds to buy inventory for a seasonal spike.

Long-Term Funding

Duration: 3-20 years.

Best for: Capital expenditure (machinery, real estate) and large-scale expansion.

Examples: Term loans, external commercial borrowings (ECBs), and private equity.

Use Case: You want to build a new warehouse or invest in long-term infrastructure.

Aman nodded. "So, short-term for cash flow issues and long-term for big moves. Makes sense."

2.4 Understanding the Cost of Capital

"Is there a way to figure out how expensive my funding will be?" Aman asked.

"Yes," Ankit smiled. "That's called the Cost of Capital—it's the total cost of using someone else's money."

Debt Cost = Interest Rate + Processing Fees + Other Charges

Equity Cost = Ownership Dilution + Future Profit Sharing

✅ *Checklist 2: Understanding Your Funding Options*

Funding Type	Collateral	Tenure	Best For
Overdraft (OD/CC)	Yes (or limited)	Ongoing	Managing cash flow gaps.
Business Loan	No	1-5 years	Quick working capital needs.
Loan Against Property (LAP)	Yes	7-15 years	Large asset-based funding.
Venture Capital	No	Equity-based	High-growth, scalable businesses.

In Summary

"So," Ankit concluded, "you now understand the key concepts—debt vs. equity, secured vs. unsecured, short-term vs. long-term, and how to calculate the cost of capital."

"Got it," Aman said confidently. "I'm starting to see which options work best for my business."

"Good," Ankit smiled. Next, we'll discuss how to **prepare your business to secure the funding** you need."

Chapter 3

Preparing for Funding – Building a Strong Case

Aman's head buzzed with the new knowledge from his conversation with Ankit. Funding no longer seemed like an impossible maze, but there was one thing still bothering him.

"Okay, Ankit," he said, settling back in his chair. "I understand the types of funding—but how do I actually convince a lender or investor to give me the money?"

Ankit grinned. "Ah, that's the most crucial part—preparing your business to look 'fund-worthy.' Let's break it down."

3.1 Why Preparation is Key to Securing Funding

"Think about it like this," Ankit began, "when a lender or investor looks at your business, they want answers to three core questions:

1. **Can you repay the money?** (For lenders)

2. **Will your business grow and deliver returns?** (For investors)

3. **Do you have a clear plan for the funds?** (For both)"

Aman laughed. "So, I need to prove I'm not a risky bet."

"Exactly. The better prepared you are, the smoother the approval process."

3.2 Financial Hygiene: Getting Your Numbers Right

"First things first—your financials need to be in order," Ankit said.

"I keep track of basic expenses," Aman shrugged.

"That won't cut it," Ankit replied. "Whether it's a bank or an investor, they want clear, reliable **financial statements.** Here's what you must prepare:

1. **Profit & Loss (P&L) Statement** – Shows revenue, expenses, and profits.

2. **Balance Sheet** – Reflects assets, liabilities, and equity.

3. **Cash Flow Statement** – Tracks money flowing in and out of the business.

4. **Bank Statements** – Last 12 months for cash flow verification.

"Investors and lenders love **clean and audited** financials," Ankit added.

✅ *Checklist 3: Financial Documentation Readiness*

Document	Prepared (Yes/No)
Profit & Loss Statement (Last 2-3 years)	

Balance Sheet (Last 2-3 years)	
Cash Flow Statement (Last 2-3 years)	
Bank Statements (12 Months)	
Income Tax Returns (2-3 years)	

3.3 Crafting a Powerful Business Plan

"Alright," Aman said, "what if my financials check out—what's next?"

"Your business plan—this is your opportunity to tell your story," Ankit explained. "Lenders want to know how you'll repay; investors want to know how you'll grow."

Your Business Plan Must Include:

1. **Executive Summary** – A quick snapshot of your business.

2. **Business Model** – How do you make money?

3. **Market Opportunity** – How big is your market? Who are your customers?

4. **Funding Need** – How much do you need and why?

5. **Repayment or Return Plan** – How will you pay back the loan or generate returns?

✅ _**Template 1: Business Plan Structure**_

Section	Description
Executive Summary	Business overview, key metrics, and funding needs
Business Model	How do you earn revenue and scale?
Market Opportunity	Industry size, customer demand, and competition
Funding Requirement	Exact amount needed and purpose
Repayment or Return Plan	How you'll repay (for debt) or deliver returns (for equity)

3.4 Strengthening Your Personal & Business Credit Profile

"Do lenders really check my **credit score**?" Aman asked.

"Absolutely," Ankit nodded. "For small businesses, banks evaluate both **business** and **personal credit**. A low credit score can block your approval."

Tips to Strengthen Your Credit Profile:

1. **Check Your Credit Report** – Ensure accuracy (CIBIL score for India).

2. **Clear Outstanding Dues** – Pay off credit card and loan balances.

3. **Maintain a Healthy Bank Balance** – Avoid frequent overdrafts.

4. **Separate Business & Personal Finances** – Use a business bank account for all transactions.

☑️ *Checklist 4: Credit Readiness*

Credit Factor	Action Status
CIBIL Score (750+ preferred)	
Personal & Business Credit Report	Reviewed and corrected (if needed)
Outstanding Loan Clearance	In progress/completed
Business Bank Account in Use	Yes/No

3.5 Preparing for the Funding Interview

"Is there an interview process for loans?" Aman asked curiously.

"For serious funding—absolutely," Ankit said. "Here's how you prepare:

1. **Know Your Numbers** – Be ready to explain revenue, costs, and margins.

2. **Justify the Ask** – Clearly explain why you need the specific amount.

3. **Address Risks** – Be upfront about risks and how you'll mitigate them.

4. **Demonstrate Growth** – Share key milestones and plans."

 ***Checklist 5: Funding Interview Prep***

Question	YourAnswer
Why do you need funding?	
How will you use the funds?	
How will you repay or deliver returns?	
What are the main risks, and how will you mitigate them?	

In Summary

"Think of securing funding like preparing for an exam," Ankit concluded. "The better prepared you are—financials, business plan, credit profile, and interview answers—the better your chances of success."

Aman leaned back, feeling a new sense of clarity. "Alright. I'm ready to do the work. What's next?"

"Next," Ankit grinned, "we'll explore specific **funding options** and how to unlock them."

★ ★ ★ ★

Chapter 4

Unlocking the Right Funding Option for Your Business

Aman arrived at the cafe a few minutes early. He was feeling more confident after organizing his financials and preparing his business plan. Today, he was eager to dive into the specifics of how to choose the best funding option for his growing business.

When Ankit walked in, Aman greeted him with a smile. "I'm ready— let's talk about where the money is and how to get it!"

Ankit laughed. "Glad to hear it. Funding isn't 'one-size-fits-all,' so we need to match the right type of funding with your business goals."

4.1 Matching Funding to Business Stages

"First," Ankit began, "the kind of funding you need depends on where your business is on its growth journey." He pulled out a notepad and drew three stages:

1. **Startup Stage** – You need capital to build, test, and launch.

2. **Growth Stage** – You need funds to scale, expand, and market.

3. **Maturity Stage** – You may need financing for working capital or acquisitions.

What Funding Works Best at Each Stage?

Business Stage	Best Funding Options	Purpose
Startup	Bootstrapping, Friends & Family, Seed Funding	Product development, market testing
Early Growth	Business Loans, Angel Investors, Government Schemes	Expanding operations, marketing
Scaling Up	Venture Capital, Revenue-Based Financing, Bank Loans	Geographic or product expansion
Maturity	Private Equity, IPO, Asset-Based Loans	Acquisitions, working capital

Aman pointed to the Growth Stage. "This is where I am—I need funding to expand operations and improve technology."

"Exactly," Ankit nodded. "Let's break down your best options."

4.2 Exploring Debt Funding Options

"Debt funding works best when you want to retain ownership and have predictable revenue," Ankit explained.

"Sounds right," Aman agreed. "What are my options?"

(a) Working Capital Loans

Best For: Managing cash flow gaps, inventory, or short-term expenses.

- **Overdraft (OD)** – Flexible withdrawal up to a limit.

- **Cash Credit (CC)** – Like an OD, but based on inventory or receivables.

Example: A retail store using a ₹100 lakh CC limit for seasonal inventory.

(b) Term Loans

Best For: Fixed, long-term investments like machinery, technology, or property.

- **Secured Term Loan** – Requires collateral; lower interest rates.

- **Unsecured Business Loan** – No collateral but higher interest.

Example: A manufacturer taking a ₹500 lakh term loan for new machinery.

✅ *Checklist 6: Debt Funding Readiness*

Requirement	Status(Prepared/Not Ready)
Clear business purpose for the loan	
Up-to-date financial records	
Credit score above 750	
Collateral availability (if required)	

4.3 Exploring Equity Funding Options

"Equity funding," Ankit explained, "means giving up a share of your business in exchange for capital. It's ideal if you want to scale fast and are willing to share ownership."

Aman tilted his head. "I'm open to it—what are the main types?"

(a) Angel Investors

Best For: Early-stage startups with high growth potential.

- Typically invest between ₹10 lakhs and ₹5 crores.

- Provide mentorship along with funding.

Example: A tech platform receiving ₹1 crore from an angel investor to expand into new cities.

(b) Venture Capital (VC)

Best For: High-growth businesses that want to scale aggressively.

- Larger investment amounts (₹2 crores to ₹100 crores+).

- Often requires rapid growth and exit strategies.

Example: A food delivery startup raising ₹50 crores to expand nationwide.

☑️ *Checklist 7: Equity Funding Readiness*

Requirement	Status (Prepared/Not Ready)
Business plan with clear growth potential	
Scalable business model	
Willingness to share ownership	
Defined exit strategy for investors	

4.4 Unlocking Government Schemes & Grants

Aman's eyes widened. "Wait—are there government programs that could help?"

"Absolutely," Ankit nodded. "In India, there are several schemes designed to support MSMEs and startups."

(a) CGTMSE (Credit Guarantee Fund Trust for Micro and Small Enterprises)

Best For: MSMEs needing collateral-free loans.

- Loans up to ₹10 crores without collateral.

- Applicable for both manufacturing and service businesses.

(b) SIDBI Schemes

Best For: Startups and MSMEs needing project-specific funding.

- **Fund of Funds for Startups (FFS)** – Supports venture capital for early-stage businesses.

- **SIDBI Term Loan** – Offers attractive rates for green and tech-based businesses.

✅ *Template 2: Government Funding Application Checklist*

Scheme	Eligibility	Documents Needed
CGTMSE	MSMEs (Manufacturing & Services)	Business plan, financials, KYC
Mudra Loan	Micro-businesses	Business proof, identity documents
SIDBI Fund	Innovative startups	Pitch deck, business plan

4.5 Alternative Funding: Beyond Traditional Options

"What if banks say no?" Aman asked.

"Good question—there are still **alternative funding** sources," Ankit said.

(a) Revenue-Based Financing (RBF)

Best For: Businesses with regular revenue but no collateral.

- Repayment is a percentage of monthly revenue.

- No fixed EMIs.

(b) Peer-to-Peer (P2P) Lending

Best For: Small businesses looking for unsecured loans.

- Fast approval with flexible terms.

- Ideal for amounts up to ₹50 lakhs.

In Summary

Ankit leaned back. "Now you understand the right funding for your business stage—from bank loans to equity and even alternative sources."

Aman grinned. "I'm feeling ready to make my move. What's next?"

"Next," Ankit said, "we'll discuss how **to present your case and increase your approval chances.**"

Chapter 5

Mastering the Funding Application Process

Aman stirred his coffee as he leaned forward, his mind buzzing with ideas. "Alright, Ankit," he said, "I know which funding options fit my business. But... how do I actually get approved? What's the secret to a successful funding application?"

Ankit smiled. "It's not magic—it's preparation and presentation. Let's break down how to craft a winning funding application."

5.1 Understanding the Lender's Mindset

"First," Ankit began, "put yourself in the lender's shoes. Whether it's a bank, an investor, or a government body, they all want three things:

1. **Clarity** – What do you need the money for?

2. **Confidence** – Can you repay or deliver returns?

3. **Compliance** – Are you meeting their requirements?"

"Got it," Aman said, nodding. "I need to be crystal clear and show I'm low-risk."

5.2 The Core Elements of a Strong Funding Application

Ankit pulled out a notepad and sketched a simple diagram.

A strong application has four pillars:

1. **Business Story** – Why does your business exist, and what makes it unique?

2. **Financial Strength** – Are your numbers accurate and promising?

3. **Clear Funding Purpose** – How will you use the money and repay it?

4. **Supportive Documents** – Are all required papers in place?

5.3 Crafting a Persuasive Business Narrative

"People connect with stories, not just numbers," Ankit said. "Your business narrative should answer three core questions:

1. What problem are you solving?

2. Why is your solution unique?

3. How will this funding drive growth?

5.4 Presenting Your Financial Strength

"Lenders and investors will **scrutinize your numbers**," Ankit warned. "Make sure your financials tell a clear, consistent story."

Key Financial Metrics to Showcase:

1. **Revenue & Growth Trends** – Steady, upward growth builds confidence.

2. **Profit Margins** – Healthy margins indicate sustainability.

3. **Debt-to-Income Ratio** – Keep this below 40% for easier loan approvals.

4. **Cash Flow Management** – Positive cash flow signals repayment ability.

5.5 Defining a Clear Funding Ask

"Be specific when asking for money," Ankit advised. "General requests raise red flags."

"Got it," Aman said. "How do I structure it?"

Formula: Funding Ask = Purpose + Amount + ROI

5.6 Preparing the Required Documentation

"No matter how strong your story is," Ankit said, "without the right paperwork, your application won't move forward."

✅ *Checklist 8: Mandatory Documentation*

Document	Required for	Status
Business Plan	Loans, Investors	
Audited Financial Statements	All Funding Types	
KYC (Aadhaar, PAN, GST)	Banks, Government	
Bank Statements (12 Months)	Loans, RBF	
Business Registration Certificate	All Funding Types	

| Collateral Documents (If Required) | Secured Loans | |

5.7 The Art of the Perfect Funding Pitch

"Your written application is vital," Ankit said, "but many lenders also want a live pitch."

Aman groaned. "I'm not a great speaker."

"You don't have to be," Ankit reassured him. "Follow this simple structure."

The 5-Minute Funding Pitch Structure:

Introduction – Who you are and what your business does.

Problem & Solution – What issue do you solve, and how?

Business Traction – Share key milestones (revenue, clients, growth).

Funding Ask – How much do you need, and how do you use it?

Future Vision – Where will this funding take your business?

5.8 Common Mistakes to Avoid

Aman scribbled notes furiously. "This is gold! What mistakes should I avoid?"

Top 5 Funding Application Mistakes:

1. **Unclear Purpose** – Vague or unrealistic funding requests.

2. **Incomplete Documentation** – Missing financial records or compliance forms.

3. **Inconsistent Financials** – Discrepancies across reports.

4. **Weak Pitch** – Failing to communicate the growth potential.

5. **Ignoring Follow-Ups** – Not tracking your application status.

In Summary

Ankit leaned back, satisfied. "A successful funding application is a mix of a clear business story, solid financials, and precise paperwork. Get this right, and your approval chances skyrocket."

Aman smiled. "I feel ready to submit my application—and actually get funded."

"Good," Ankit said. "Next, we'll tackle **navigating the funding approval process** and what happens after you apply."

Chapter 6

Navigating the Funding Approval Process

Aman's funding application was finally ready. With a sense of accomplishment, he handed the neatly prepared documents to Ankit. "This feels solid," he said. "But what happens next? How does the approval process actually work?"

Ankit smiled, sipping his coffee. "Great question. Once you apply, the real work begins on the lender's side. Let's walk through what happens behind the scenes—and how you can improve your chances of getting a quick 'yes.'"

6.1 The Funding Approval Journey: Step-by-Step

"Different lenders follow different timelines," Ankit explained. "But the general approval process has five key stages."

The 5 Stages of Funding Approval

1. **Application Submission** – Providing documents and the funding request.

2. **Preliminary Screening** – Quick review for basic eligibility and completeness.

3. **Credit Evaluation** – In-depth analysis of your financials and repayment capacity.

4. **Decision & Sanction** – Approval, modification, or rejection of your request.

5. **Disbursement** – Release of funds once formalities are complete.

Aman raised an eyebrow. "Sounds thorough. How long does it usually take?"

"For traditional banks," Ankit said, "it can take 1-4 weeks. Private lenders and alternative funding options are faster—sometimes as quick as 2-10 days if your paperwork is right."

6.2 What Happens During the Credit Evaluation?

"This is the most critical phase," Ankit explained. "Lenders go deep into your business to assess risk and repayment ability."

Key Factors Lenders Evaluate:

Financial Health – Revenue, profitability, cash flow.

Creditworthiness – CIBIL/business credit score (750+ is ideal).

Collateral (if applicable) – Market value and legal validity of assets.

Business Viability – Market potential and operational efficiency.

Management Profile – Your expertise and track record.

Aman frowned. "What if my credit score isn't perfect?"

"You can still secure funding," Ankit reassured him. "But be ready to offer collateral or explain any discrepancies clearly."

6.3 How to Handle Lender Queries & Clarifications

"Lenders often come back with follow-up questions," Ankit said. "Responding quickly and clearly shows you're professional and prepared."

Common Lender Queries:

1. **Purpose Clarification** – Why exactly do you need the funds?

2. **Financial Explanation** – Address inconsistencies in revenue or expenses.

3. **Collateral Documentation** – Provide clear title deeds and valuations.

4. **Business Model Proof** – Evidence of customer traction or operational success.

Aman sighed. "That sounds like a lot of back-and-forth."

"It can be," Ankit admitted, "but having a response strategy helps."

Potential Query	Your Prepared Response
Purpose of Loan	
Addressing Financial Gaps	
Collateral Documentation	
Future Revenue Projections	

6.4 Dealing with Conditional Approvals

"Sometimes," Ankit continued, "lenders approve funding with conditions attached. These could be minor or significant."

Common Approval Conditions:

1. **Personal Guarantee** – You back the loan.

2. **Additional Collateral** – Extra assets for security.

3. **Usage Monitoring** – Funds must be used for specified purposes.

4. **Financial Covenants** – Maintain specific financial ratios.

Aman asked, "Can I negotiate these conditions?"

"Absolutely," Ankit nodded. "If your case is strong, you can request better terms—especially on interest rates and collateral."

✅ *Template 3: Negotiating Funding Terms*

Condition	Your Negotiation Plan
Interest Rate	Request a 0.5-1% reduction if possible
Collateral	Limit to specific assets only.
Prepayment Penalty	Ask for a waiver or reduced charges.
Reporting Requirements	Request annual vs. quarterly reports.

6.5 Managing Rejections & Next Steps

"What if I'm rejected?" Aman asked nervously.

"It happens," Ankit said calmly. "The key is to analyze why and pivot accordingly."

Top Reasons for Funding Rejection:

1. **Weak Financials** – Inconsistent revenue or poor cash flow.

2. **Poor Credit History** – Low CIBIL score or past defaults.

3. **Unclear Business Plan** – Weak growth strategy or unclear goals.

4. **Inadequate Documentation** – Missing key records or incorrect details.

✅ Checklist 10: Post-Rejection Action Plan

Reason for Rejection	Your Next Step
Financial Weakness	Strengthen cash flow & revenue trends
Credit Score Issues	Improve credit and seek alternative funding.
Documentation Gaps	Organize complete records for resubmission.
Business Model Concerns	Refine the plan & provide stronger evidence.

6.6 Preparing for Fund Disbursement

"When your funding is approved, you're almost there," Ankit said. "But there are final steps before you receive the money."

Disbursement Checklist:

1. **Sign Loan/Investment Agreement** – Carefully review all terms.

2. **Submit Final KYC & Compliance Docs** – Ensure all legalities are met.

3. **Open Designated Bank Account** – If required for fund tracking.

4. **Confirm Disbursement Schedule** – Know when and how funds arrive.

In Summary

Aman leaned back, satisfied. "I had no idea there was so much happening behind the scenes."

"Most people don't," Ankit said with a grin. "But now you know how to navigate every step—from submission to disbursement. You're ahead of the game."

Aman smiled. "I'm feeling ready. What's next?"

"Next," Ankit said, "we'll explore how to use the funds effectively and ensure long-term business success."

Chapter 7

Managing & Maximizing Your Funding

Aman leaned back in his chair, a smile creeping across his face. "Finally!" he said. "I've got the approval email. But now comes the tricky part—how do I make the most of it?"

Ankit nodded, his expression serious. "Getting funded is just the beginning, Aman. How you use the money determines whether you scale up or stumble."

7.1 The Mindset Shift: From Borrower to Growth Strategist

"Most people make a big mistake after getting funded," Ankit explained. "They treat the money like a windfall instead of a growth tool."

"So, what should my mindset be?" Aman asked.

"Think like an investor in your own business. Every rupee should work toward expanding revenue or improving efficiency."

✅ *Checklist 11: Your Funding Utilization Mindset*

Principle	Your Strategy
Treat funding as a growth tool.	Focus on revenue-generating activities.
Prioritize ROI	Invest where you see the highest returns.

| Control spending | Avoid unnecessary expenses or lifestyle creep. |
| Track every rupee | Set up clear monitoring systems. |

7.2 Crafting a Smart Fund Utilization Plan

Aman leaned forward. "Okay, I get it—be strategic. But how do I decide where to allocate the money?"

"Break it down," Ankit said, grabbing a piece of paper. "Use this simple model: Revenue, Efficiency, and Compliance."

The 3 Pillars of Smart Fund Utilization

1. **Revenue Growth** – Marketing, product development, and new markets.

2. **Operational Efficiency** – Technology upgrades, automation, supply chain.

3. **Compliance & Risk Management** – GST, tax filings, legal formalities.

☑ *Template 4: Fund Allocation Plan*

Category	Amount (₹)	Expected Impact
Marketing & Customer Acquisition		Increase revenue by ___%
Technology & Process Automation		Reduce costs by ___%

Inventory or Equipment		Increase production capacity by ___%
Compliance & Legal Fees		Ensure smooth regulatory operations.

7.3 Managing Cash Flow After Funding

"Cash flow can still sink a business—even after funding," Ankit warned.

Aman frowned. "But I thought funding solves cash problems."

"It does," Ankit said, "but only if you manage inflows and outflows carefully."

Golden Rules of Cash Flow Management:

1. **Separate Funds** – Keep the loan in a dedicated account.

2. **Prioritize High-Return Expenses** – Focus on activities that boost revenue.

3. **Maintain a Cash Buffer** – Set aside at least 3 months of expenses.

4. **Review Monthly** – Track and adjust your spending every 30 days.

7.4 Monitoring Fund Utilization

Aman scribbled down notes. "I need to stay on top of every rupee. Any tools that help with that?"

"Absolutely," Ankit replied. "**Start with fund utilization reports**. These help track where every rupee goes—and they're essential if you're raising more capital later."

Fund utilization reports aren't just about accountability—they're your roadmap for financial discipline. Here's what they typically include:

- Breakup of fund usage (e.g., marketing, tech, salaries)

- Variance analysis (planned vs. actual spend)

- Milestone tracking (what goals the spending has achieved)

- Cash burn rate

7.5 Maximizing Returns: What Successful Businesses Do Differently

"What separates businesses that scale from those that struggle?" Aman asked.

"Execution," Ankit said. "Smart founders know how to turn capital into growth. Here's how they do it."

5 Best Practices of Funded Businesses:

1. **Invest in Talent** – Hire specialists for key growth areas.

2. **Leverage Technology** – Automate where possible to save time and money.

3. **Track Key Metrics** – Monitor ROI on every rupee spent.

4. **Stay Agile** – Adjust your strategy based on real-time data.

5. **Communicate with Stakeholders** – Keep investors or lenders updated regularly.

7.6 Avoiding Common Post-Funding Mistakes

Aman's pen hovered over his notebook. "What should I not do with the funds?"

Ankit chuckled. "Glad you asked. Avoid these traps if you want your business to thrive."

5 Common Post-Funding Mistakes:

1. **Over-Spending on Non-Essentials** – Avoid fancy offices or unnecessary perks.

2. **Ignoring Compliance** – Stay updated with taxes and regulations.

3. **Weak Reporting** – Always maintain transparent financials.

4. **Unplanned Expansion** – Scale only when your processes are strong.

5. **Poor Communication** – Keep lenders or investors in the loop.

☑ *Template 5: Funding Risk Mitigation Plan*

Risk	Mitigation Strategy
Over-Spending	Set strict budgets and track expenses.
Compliance Lapses	Regularly audit your legal and tax position.
Weak Reporting	Implement monthly financial reporting.
Over-Expansion	Validate new markets before scaling.

In Summary

Ankit closed his notebook. "Funding is fuel, but you need to drive the vehicle responsibly. Plan well, track closely, and always prioritize growth over glamour."

Aman smiled. "I've got a clear roadmap. I'm ready to make every rupee work for me."

"Perfect," Ankit said. "Next, we'll dive into **building long-term lender and investor relationships**—because one round of funding is just the beginning."

Chapter 8

Building Long-Term Relationships with Lenders & Investors

Aman walked into the café, his face lit up with excitement. "Ankit, things are moving fast! I'm managing the funds well, but I keep hearing that relationships with lenders and investors are crucial for future funding. What's the secret?"

Ankit smiled. "You're absolutely right. One loan or investment isn't the end—it's just the beginning. If you build strong, trust-based relationships, future funding becomes much easier. Let's break down how to do that."

8.1 Why Long-Term Relationships Matter

"So why is relationship-building such a big deal?" Aman asked, sipping his coffee.

"Because lenders and investors don't just fund business models—they fund people they trust," Ankit explained. "Strong relationships lead to better terms, faster approvals, and access to bigger opportunities."

✅ Checklist 12: The Benefits of Strong Financial Relationships

Benefit	How It Helps Your Business
Easier Access to Future Funding	Faster approvals and larger credit limits.
Better Loan Terms	Lower interest rates and relaxed conditions.
Credibility & Reputation	Builds trust with new investors or banks.
Growth Partnerships	Access to new markets and strategic advice.
Emergency Support	Quick assistance during cash flow issues.

8.2 Understanding the Lender's & Investor's Mindset

"Alright," Aman said, "I'm in. But how do I think like a lender or investor?"

"Great question," Ankit replied. "Here's what's on their mind when working with you."

What Lenders Care About:

1. **Repayment Ability** – Can you pay on time?

2. **Financial Discipline** – Are your records clean and updated?

3. **Transparency** – Do you share information openly?

What Investors Care About:

1. **Scalability** – Can your business grow 5x-10x?

2. **Return on Investment (ROI)** – What's the potential payout?

3. **Founder's Commitment** – Are you fully invested in your business?

8.3 Building Trust: Your Communication Blueprint

"So," Aman asked, "what's the best way to communicate with them?"

"Simple—be proactive, transparent, and consistent," Ankit said. "Here's your blueprint."

☑ **Template 6: Lender & Investor Communication Plan**

Frequency	What to Share	Purpose
Monthly Update	Financial performance, cash flow, KPIs	Build confidence and transparency
Quarterly Review	Key business milestones, future plans	Show progress and vision
Annual Report	Complete financials, projections	Strengthen long-term trust
Ad-Hoc Communication	Challenges, pivots, opportunities	Maintain open dialogue

8.4 Handling Challenges Transparently

Aman leaned back, frowning. "What if things go wrong? How do I explain setbacks without losing their trust?"

"Never hide problems," Ankit said firmly. "Lenders and investors know that business has risks. They care more about how you handle those risks."

How to Share Bad News Effectively:

1. **Be Prompt** – Share issues early before they escalate.

2. **Stay Solution-Focused** – Present the problem and your action plan.

3. **Own It** – Take responsibility for mistakes.

☑ **Template 7: Issue Reporting Framework**

1. **What Happened:** (Describe the challenge clearly)

2. **Why It Happened:** (Root cause analysis)

3. **Action Plan:** (Steps to resolve the issue)

4. **Expected Timeline:** (By when will it be fixed?)

5. **Support Needed:** (If you require assistance or flexibility)

8.5 Strengthening Relationships Beyond Money

"So, it's more than just paying on time?" Aman asked.

"Absolutely," Ankit said. "Strong relationships go beyond transactions. Involve them in your journey."

✅ Checklist 13: Ways to Deepen Relationships

Action	Impact
Invite to Business Milestones	Strengthens personal connection
Share Market Insights	Positions you as an industry expert
Appreciate Their Support	Builds goodwill and loyalty
Seek Their Advice Occasionally	Shows respect for their expertise
Introduce New Opportunities	Creates mutual growth prospects

8.6 Preparing for Future Rounds of Funding

Aman's eyes widened. "Okay, I've built great relationships—how do I prepare for my next big round?"

Ankit chuckled. "It starts now. Keep your business 'funding-ready' at all times."

✅ Template 8: Future Funding Readiness Plan

[Task	Status (In Progress/Done)
Maintain Updated Financial Reports	
Track Key Performance Metrics	
Build a Clear Growth Narrative	
Keep Compliance Documentation Ready	

In Summary

Ankit leaned back. "Aman, funding is not just a transaction—it's a relationship. Treat lenders and investors like partners, and they'll stand by you through every stage of growth."

Aman smiled. "Got it. I'll nurture these relationships the way I nurture my business. What's next?"

"Next," Ankit said, "we'll dive into the art of **innovating and growing beyond the first round of funding**."

Chapter 9

Innovating & Growing Beyond the First Funding Round

Aman leaned back in his chair, a thoughtful look on his face. "Ankit, I get it—funding is crucial. But once I've secured my first round, how do I keep the momentum going? I've seen businesses grow fast, but then they hit a wall."

Ankit nodded. "That's because many entrepreneurs stop innovating after their first round of funding. But the real winners? They treat funding as a launchpad, not a finish line. Let's dive into how you can keep innovating, stay competitive, and secure future funding."

9.1 Why Innovation is Essential Post-Funding

Aman raised an eyebrow. "Why is innovation so critical after funding? Isn't the hard part over?"

Ankit smiled. "Not quite. Investors fund you because they believe in your potential, but they expect you to grow faster and smarter. Without innovation, you risk stagnation. Here's why it matters."

☑ Checklist 14: Why You Must Keep Innovating

Reason	Impact
Stay Competitive	Keeps you ahead of emerging players
Improve Profit Margins	Optimizes processes and cuts costs
Attract Future Investors	Positions your business for the next funding round
Diversify Revenue Streams	Reduces risk from relying on a single product
Enhance Customer Loyalty	Keeps customers engaged and increases lifetime value

9.2 Identifying Innovation Opportunities

Aman tapped his pen. "So, how do I find areas to innovate? My resources are limited."

"Simple," Ankit said. "Look at your customers, operations, and market trends. The best innovations solve real problems efficiently."

3 Key Areas to Focus Your Innovation Efforts:

1. **Product Innovation** – Improve or expand your offerings.

2. **Process Innovation** – Streamline operations for better efficiency.

3. **Business Model Innovation** – Explore new revenue channels or customer segments.

9.3 Using Funding to Drive Innovation

Aman leaned forward. "Okay, I have ideas—but how do I allocate funds without running out of cash?"

"You need a funding allocation strategy, Aman. It's about balancing your spending on innovation while maintaining financial discipline."

✅ Checklist 15: Smart Fund Allocation for Innovation

Area	Recommended % of Funds
Core Business Operations	40%–50 % (Maintain existing functions)
Innovation Initiatives	20%–30% (Test and launch new ideas)
Marketing & Expansion	15%–20% (Scale successful innovations)
Reserve Fund	10% (Prepare for unexpected needs)

9.4 Securing Additional Funding for Growth

Aman nodded. "This makes sense. But when I need more funding for the next stage, where should I look?"

"Great question," Ankit said. "Your options expand as your business grows. Here are some funding avenues after your first round."

✅ Template 9: Post-Funding Capital Options

Funding Source	Ideal For	Key Advantage
Venture Capital (Series A, B)	High-growth, scalable businesses	Larger funding amounts, strategic support
Revenue-Based Financing	Businesses with steady revenue	No equity dilution
Government Grants & Schemes	Innovation-driven or social impact projects	Non-repayable capital
Corporate Partnerships	Businesses complementing large corporations	Access to expertise and distribution
Convertible Debt	Bridge financing between equity rounds	Delay equity dilution

9.5 Monitoring Key Growth Metrics

Aman scribbled notes. "If I want future investors, what metrics do they care about?"

Ankit smiled. "Investors love data-driven stories. Here's what you should track."

✅ Checklist 16: Key Metrics for Long-Term Growth

Metric	Why It Matters
Monthly Recurring Revenue (MRR)	Shows consistent revenue generation
Customer Acquisition Cost (CAC)	Measures how efficiently you attract customers

Lifetime Value (LTV)	Indicates long-term customer profitability
Gross Margin	Reflects operational efficiency
Burn Rate & Runway	Shows how long you can sustain operations
Churn Rate	Monitors customer retention

9.6 Leveraging Partnerships for Innovation

Aman scratched his chin. "This sounds like a lot to manage alone. Can partnerships help?"

"Absolutely," Ankit nodded. "Strategic partnerships provide capital, expertise, and market access—without needing to give up too much equity."

✅ Template 10: Partnership Development Framework

Step	Action
Identify Potential Partners	Look for complementary businesses
Align Objectives	Ensure shared goals and values.
Structure Win-Win Deals	Define clear terms and mutual benefits.
Measure Outcomes	Set KPIs to track success.

In Summary

Ankit smiled as he wrapped up. "Aman, your first round of funding is just the beginning. To stay ahead:

1. **Keep innovating**—in products, processes, and business models.

2. **Allocate funds wisely** to balance stability and experimentation.

3. **Track key metrics** to show investors you're on a sustainable path.

Do this consistently, and you won't just survive—you'll thrive."

Aman's eyes sparkled with clarity. "I'm ready to play the long game. What's next?"

Ankit chuckled. "Next, we will see alternative funding sources available."

Chapter 10

Unlocking Alternative Funding Sources

Aman and Ankit were sitting at their favorite café, the aroma of fresh coffee filling the air. Aman stirred his cup thoughtfully. "Ankit, I get the usual funding methods—bank loans, credit lines—but what about other ways to raise capital? Sometimes, traditional lenders move too slowly."

Ankit smiled. "You're right. Many businesses miss out because they only think of banks. But the world of alternative funding is vast—and can offer faster, more flexible options."

Aman leaned in, intrigued. "I'm listening. What are my options?"

10.1 Why Explore Alternative Funding?

"Why bother with alternatives when banks offer so much?" Aman asked.

"Simple," Ankit said. "Sometimes, speed, flexibility, or custom solutions matter more than low interest rates. Alternative funding can provide:

- **Faster access to capital** when time is critical.

- **Customized repayment structures** tailored to your cash flow.

- **Options when traditional financing isn't available**, like for new businesses."

✅ Checklist 17: When to Consider Alternative Funding

Situation	Why It Works
Urgent cash flow needs	Faster approval and disbursement
High growth or expansion	Flexible repayment and larger amounts
No collateral available	Unsecured options like revenue-based loans
Early-stage startup	Access to investors, grants, and crowdfunding
Rejected by traditional banks	Alternative lenders offer wider criteria.

Aman nodded. "Got it. So, what are the main alternative funding types I should know?"

10.2 Exploring Key Alternative Funding Options

Ankit pulled out his notebook. "Let's break it down by type—each has its own benefits and ideal use cases."

✅ Template 11: Alternative Funding Options Overview

Funding Type	How It Works	Ideal For
Invoice Discounting	Get cash upfront by selling unpaid invoices	Businesses with delayed payments
Revenue-Based Financing	Repay as a percentage of monthly revenue	Businesses with steady cash flow

Angel Investors	Equity investment from high-net-worth individuals	Early-stage, high-growth startups
Crowdfunding	Raise small amounts from many people online	Product launches or innovative ideas
Grants & Government Schemes	Non-repayable funding for specific industries	R&D, tech startups, MSMEs
Private Lenders/NBFCs	Quicker loans with flexible terms	Businesses needing faster funding

Aman raised an eyebrow. "Invoice discounting—how does that work exactly?"

10.3 Understanding Invoice Discounting & Factoring

Ankit explained, "If you've issued invoices to clients but are waiting on payment, you can sell those invoices to a lender who advances 80-90% of the value immediately."

✅ Checklist 18: Is Invoice Discounting Right for You?

- Do you have unpaid invoices from creditworthy clients?

- Is cash flow your main challenge?

- Are you okay with a small discount fee for immediate cash?

Aman nodded. "Sounds perfect for handling delayed customer payments. What's next?"

10.4 Leveraging Revenue-Based Financing

Ankit continued, "Instead of fixed EMIs, revenue-based financing lets you repay as a **percentage of your monthly revenue**—ideal if your income fluctuates."

☑ **Template 12: Revenue-Based Financing Model**

Metric	Example
Funding Amount	₹up to 2 Crores
Revenue Share Percentage	10% of monthly revenue
Repayment Cap	Example- 1.3x of principal
Monthly Payment	Varies based on your revenue

Aman's eyes widened. "So, in slower months, I pay less?"

"Exactly," Ankit confirmed. "It aligns repayment with your business cycle."

10.5 Tapping Into Angel Investors & Private Equity

"What about bringing in outside investors?" Aman asked.

"Great question," Ankit said, "Angel investors provide early-stage capital in exchange for equity. It's best if you're scaling fast and need strategic support."

☑ **Checklist 19: Preparing to Pitch Angel Investors**

1. Clear **business model** and growth plan.

2. Solid **financials** with future projections.

3. Defined **equity offer**—how much are you willing to give?

4. A compelling **pitch deck** that tells your story.

5. **Exit strategy**—how will investors get returns?

Aman scratched his head. "But won't that dilute my ownership?"

"Yes—but the right investor can accelerate growth beyond what you could do alone," Ankit said.

10.6 Utilizing Crowdfunding Platforms

"And crowdfunding?" Aman asked.

"It's raising small amounts from many backers through platforms like Kickstarter or Indian alternatives like Ketto," Ankit explained.

☑ **Template 13: Crowdfunding Success Strategy**

Step	Action
Create a Story	Clearly explain your business idea/mission
Set Funding Goal	Be realistic but ambitious.
Offer Rewards	Provide incentives (products, services)

Market Aggressively	Use social media and PR to drive traffic.
Engage Backers	Communicate regularly to build trust.

Aman chuckled. "So, if I have a compelling story, I can raise funds without giving up equity?"

"Exactly," Ankit smiled.

10.7 Accessing Government Grants & Schemes

Aman tapped the table. "What about government schemes? Are they practical?"

"They are if you qualify," Ankit replied. "Grants and subsidized loans can ease your funding needs—but they require strict compliance."

✅ **Checklist 20: Navigating Government Schemes**

1. Identify relevant schemes for your business (e.g., MSME loans).

2. Ensure you meet the eligibility criteria.

3. Prepare a strong business proposal.

4. Maintain documentation—audits, GST records, and tax filings.

Aman sighed. "It sounds like a lot—but free money is hard to ignore."

"Exactly," Ankit agreed. "It's worth the effort if you want low-cost capital."

In Summary

Ankit leaned back. "Alternative funding opens doors when traditional options aren't a fit. Each option has its place—use what aligns with your business stage and needs."

1. **Invoice Discounting**: Fast cash flow from unpaid invoices.

2. **Revenue-Based Financing**: Flexible repayments tied to revenue.

3. **Angel Investors**: Equity in exchange for early-stage funding.

4. **Crowdfunding**: Raise capital from the public.

5. **Government Schemes**: Grants and low-interest loans.

Aman smiled. "With these tools, I have options—no more feeling stuck!"

Ankit nodded. "Exactly. Now we will deep dive into **various international funding options.**"

Chapter 11

Leveraging International Funding Opportunities

Aman and Ankit found themselves at a business networking event, surrounded by entrepreneurs discussing opportunities beyond India's borders. As they sipped on their Coffee, Aman leaned toward Ankit.

"A lot of these startups talk about getting funding from international investors. Is that even an option for a business like mine?" he asked curiously.

Ankit smiled. "Absolutely. International funding isn't just for tech giants—it's a powerful tool for businesses looking to scale. With the right approach, you can tap into a world of capital beyond Indian borders."

11.1 Why Consider International Funding?

Aman furrowed his brow. "But why would a foreign investor care about a small business like mine?"

Ankit explained, "Global investors look for promising businesses in emerging markets like India. Plus, international funding often provides:

- **Larger capital pools**—more funds than local sources.

- **Global networks**—access to new markets and expertise.

- **Competitive terms**—lower interest or more flexible repayment.

If your business has export potential, technology, or a unique model, you're a prime candidate."

✅ **Checklist 21: Are You Ready for International Funding?**

1. Do you have a **scalable business model** that could work globally?

2. Are you comfortable meeting **international compliance** standards?

3. Is your business eligible under **FEMA** (Foreign Exchange Management Act) regulations?

4. Do you have a **clear expansion plan** to show global growth?

Aman nodded slowly. "Okay, I'm interested. What are my options?"

11.2 Key International Funding Sources

Ankit pulled out a notebook. "Here are the most practical international funding sources for Indian businesses:"

☑ Template 14: International Funding Options Overview

Funding Source	Description	Ideal For
Foreign Direct Investment (FDI)	Equity investment from foreign entities	Businesses seeking long-term investors
External Commercial Borrowings (ECBs)	Loans from foreign banks and financial institutions	Infrastructure, manufacturing, and large projects
International Venture Capital	Funding from global VC firms for high-growth startups	Tech-driven and scalable businesses
Grants & Development Funds	Non-repayable funds for impact-driven projects	Renewable energy, social enterprises
Export Credit Agencies (ECAs)	Financing for businesses expanding via exports	Exporters or businesses with global sales

Aman's eyes lit up. "So, even small businesses can access these funds?"

"Absolutely," Ankit nodded. "If you position yourself right."

11.3 Understanding Foreign Direct Investment (FDI)

"What's the deal with FDI?" Aman asked.

"FDI means a foreign investor buys equity in your business. It's regulated under FEMA, but it's one of the most stable ways to raise global capital," Ankit explained.

✅ **Checklist 22: FDI Readiness Assessment**

- Do you have a **registered entity** eligible to accept foreign capital?

- Is your business in an **FDI-permitted sector** (e.g., manufacturing, tech, services)?

- Are you prepared for **due diligence** on financial and legal compliance?

- Have you created an **investment proposal** with clear growth projections?

Aman scribbled notes. "And ECBs? I've heard of those."

11.4 Leveraging External Commercial Borrowings (ECBs)

Ankit nodded. "Yes, ECBs are loans from foreign lenders like international banks, offered at competitive rates. They're ideal for businesses needing large-scale capital without giving up equity."

✅ **Template 15: ECB Snapshot**

Criteria	Details
Eligible Borrowers	Companies in manufacturing and infrastructure
Loan Currency	USD, EUR, or other foreign currencies
Minimum Maturity	3 to 5 years, depending on the loan purpose

Approval Process	Automatic route for certain sectors; RBI approval otherwise

Aman frowned. "Isn't it complex?"

"It can be," Ankit admitted. "But with the right documentation and an RBI-compliant structure, it's a cost-effective way to access global liquidity."

11.5 International Venture Capital & Angel Networks

Aman leaned forward. "What about foreign VCs? Can Indian startups really get their attention?"

"Yes!" Ankit said, "Global venture funds actively seek investments in emerging markets. Indian startups, especially in tech, fintech, and consumer products, are hot targets."

✅ Checklist 23: Preparing for International VC Funding

1. **Global Appeal** – Does your business model work outside India?

2. **Scalable Technology** – Can you scale operations across countries?

3. **Financial Projections** – Do you have a 3-5 year plan for expansion?

4. **Legal Structure** – Ensure compliance with FEMA and SEBI norms.

5. **Investor Fit** – Target VCs investing in your sector and geography.

Aman grinned. "Sounds promising. What about free money—grants?"

11.6 Unlocking Global Grants & Development Funds

"Grants are non-repayable but come with conditions," Ankit explained. "Organizations like the World Bank, Asian Development Bank, and UN agencies offer them for businesses focused on social, environmental, or technological innovation."

☑ Template 16: Global Grant Strategy

Grant Provider	Focus Area
World Bank Group	Infrastructure, rural development
Bill & Melinda Gates Foundation	Healthcare, education innovations
Export-Import Bank of India (EXIM)	Export-related projects
European Union Grants	Climate action, digital transformation

Aman shook his head in amazement. "I had no idea so many opportunities were out there."

11.7 How to Approach International Investors

"So," Aman asked, "how do I start approaching these investors?"

Ankit laid out a simple process:

1. **Research Target Markets** – Identify investors aligned with your sector.

2. **Prepare a Global Pitch Deck** – Tailor your pitch for **international expectations**.

3. **Engage with Global Networks** – Use platforms like **AngelList, LinkedIn**, and international accelerators.

4. **Legal & Compliance Check** – Ensure readiness under **Indian and international laws**.

✅ **Checklist 24: International Pitch Deck Essentials**

- Business Overview – Clear, concise, and globally relevant.

- Market Opportunity – Showcase your market's growth potential.

- Financial Model – Detailed and in **foreign currency**.

- Exit Strategy – Explain how investors will get their returns.

In Summary

Aman leaned back, his mind buzzing with possibilities.

"So, international funding isn't just for tech unicorns—it's accessible if I play my cards right," he said.

"Exactly," Ankit confirmed. "By understanding the options and preparing thoroughly, you can tap into global capital to scale your business like never before."

Key Takeaways:

1. **FDI**: Ideal for long-term capital via equity.

2. **ECBs**: Low-interest international loans for large projects.

3. **International VCs**: For scalable, globally focused startups.

4. **Grants**: Non-repayable funds for impactful projects.

Aman smiled. "It's time to take my business global."

Ankit raised his coffee. "To new horizons!" Now, let's explore **building a pitch for an investor.**

Chapter 12

Building a Winning Pitch for Investors

Aman and Ankit sat across from each other at their favorite café. The buzz of conversation surrounded them, but Aman's mind was fixated on one thing—his upcoming meeting with a potential investor.

"I'm nervous, Ankit," Aman admitted. "I know my business inside out, but pitching to an investor feels... intimidating."

Ankit smiled reassuringly. "That's normal. But a strong pitch isn't about dazzling them with fancy slides—it's about telling a clear, compelling story. Let's break it down step by step."

12.1 Why a Strong Pitch Matters

Aman leaned in. "Why is the pitch such a big deal? Can't the numbers speak for themselves?"

"They do," Ankit nodded, "but investors get hundreds of pitches. A great pitch grabs attention, tells your story, and makes them want to be part of your journey."

He continued, "Your pitch is your first impression—and in the funding world, that first impression can mean the difference between a handshake and a rejection."

✅ **Checklist 25: What Investors Want to Hear**

1. **Clarity** – Can you explain your business in **simple terms**?

2. **Opportunity** – Is there a **growing market** for your solution?

3. **Scalability** – Can your business **grow quickly** with more capital?

4. **Financial Returns** – How will investors **profit** from their investment?

5. **Team Strength** – Do you have a **capable team** to execute the plan?

12.2 Crafting Your Investor Pitch: The Core Structure

"Alright," Aman said, "How do I structure my pitch?"

Ankit opened his notebook and sketched out a simple outline.

"Follow this structure—it's proven to work:"

✅ **Template 17: Winning Pitch Structure**

1. **Introduction** – Who you are and why you're here.

2. **Problem Statement** – What pain point are you solving?

3. **Your Solution** – How does your business address this problem?

4. **Market Opportunity** – How big is the market? Is it growing?

5. **Business Model** – How do you make money?

6. **Traction & Milestones** – What progress have you made so far?

7. **Financial Projections** – What returns can the investor expect?

8. **Funding Ask** – How much are you raising, and how will you use it?

9. **Your Team** – Who is leading the charge?

10. **Closing** – A compelling call-to-action for investment.

Aman scribbled it down. "Sounds logical. But how much detail do I share?"

"Enough to excite them," Ankit said. "Don't drown them in data—keep it crisp and clear."

12.3 Telling a Story Investors Can't Ignore

Aman frowned. "What do you mean by 'story'? Isn't this about facts and figures?"

"Facts matter," Ankit agreed. "But investors connect with stories. Share your why—why you started, why this matters, and why now is the right time."

He leaned in. "For example, instead of saying 'We sell eco-friendly packaging,' say— 'I started this because I saw thousands of plastic packages clogging our waterways. Our product replaces plastic with biodegradable solutions, and in just one year, we've saved over 100 tons of plastic waste."

✅ **Checklist 26: Crafting Your Story**

1. **Personal Hook** – Why did you start this business?

2. **Emotional Appeal** – What problem are you passionate about solving?

3. **Urgency** – Why is **now** the right time for your business?

Aman smiled. "I get it—facts tell, but stories sell."

12.4 Financial Projections: Speaking the Investor's Language

"But what about the numbers?" Aman asked. "Investors love numbers."

"True," Ankit said. "Be realistic but ambitious. Investors want to see a clear path to profitability and a return on investment (ROI)."

✅ **Template 18: Financial Snapshot**

Year	Revenue (₹)	Expenses (₹)	Profit (₹)	ROI (%)
Year 1 (Current)	1 Cr	80 Lakh	20 Lakh	—
Year 2	2.5 Cr	1.8 Cr	70 Lakh	35%
Year 3	5 Cr	3.5 Cr	1.5 Cr	45%

"Show how your business will **scale** with the investor's funds," Ankit explained.

12.5 Delivering a Pitch with Confidence

Aman sighed. "I'm not the best public speaker. What if I mess up?"

"Practice is everything," Ankit reassured him. "Here's how to deliver your pitch like a pro:"

✅ Checklist 27: Pitch Delivery Essentials

1. **Know Your Numbers** – Be ready to explain every figure confidently.

2. **Keep It Short** – Aim for **8-12 minutes** for your core pitch.

3. **Engage, Don't Lecture** – Make eye contact and encourage questions.

4. **Anticipate Objections** – Prepare answers for tough questions.

5. **Close Strong** – End with a clear, confident ask.

Aman exhaled. "Okay, I'm feeling more prepared. But what if they say no?"

12.6 Handling Investor Objections & Rejections

Ankit smiled. "Rejection is part of the game. Instead of fearing it, learn from it."

✅ **Template 19: Common Investor Objections & Responses**

Objection	Response Strategy
"Your market is too small."	Show **data** proving future market growth.
"Your valuation is too high."	Explain the **traction** justifying your value.
"I'm not sure about your team."	Emphasize your team's **skills and experience**.
"What's your exit strategy?"	Share how investors can **profit** via acquisition or IPO.

"Every 'no' gets you closer to a 'yes,'" Ankit said. "Refine your pitch after each meeting."

In Summary

As they stood to leave, Aman's nerves had faded. "Thanks, Ankit. I feel like I can do this now."

"You absolutely can," Ankit said. "A clear, confident pitch can open doors you never imagined."

Key Takeaways:

1. **Clarity & Structure** – Keep your pitch simple and well-organized.

2. **Storytelling** – Connect emotionally while showing business value.

3. **Financials** – Present **realistic**, ambitious growth projections.

4. **Delivery** – Practice until your pitch feels **natural and** confident.

Aman smiled. "This was gold. But now I'm wondering—what if I'm not looking for investors? What if I need funds for personal goals—like buying a home, covering medical needs, or planning a wedding?"

Ankit leaned back, grinning. "Then it's time we talk about **personal loans—not for pitching, but for life planning.**

Chapter 13

Funding Life Goals – Smart Loans Beyond Business

The next day, Aman and Ankit met again—this time in Ankit's office. Aman looked curious, flipping through the notes from their last discussion.

"Ankit, yesterday we discussed investor pitches. But not everyone's looking for VC money," Aman said. "What if someone just needs funds for personal goals—like buying a house, handling an emergency, or even a gold loan?"

Ankit smiled. "Good question. Not all funding is about startups. Sometimes, we need money for life's milestones—and for that, personal loans step in."

13.1 Understanding Personal Loans

"So, personal loans are just money for personal use?" Aman asked.

"Exactly," Ankit nodded. "They can be unsecured like a personal loan or secured like a home or gold loan. Each serves a purpose."

✅ **Checklist 28: When to Consider a Personal Loan**

1. Do you have a clear reason and repayment plan?

2. Is your credit score 700+?

3. Have you compared interest rates across lenders?

4. Can your income support the EMI?

13.2 Personal Loans – For Quick & Flexible Needs

"I've heard personal loans are easy but expensive," Aman said.

"True," Ankit replied. "They're great for weddings, travel, or emergencies—but use them wisely."

Benefits:

- No collateral needed

- Fast processing (24–72 hours)

- Flexible usage

- Short tenure (1–5 years)

Note: Interest rates range from 10% to 18%.

13.3 Home Loans – Your Key to Ownership

"I'm planning to buy a flat next year," Aman said. "How do home loans work?"

"Home loans are long-term," Ankit explained. "But they come with tax benefits and help build an asset."

Benefits:

- Lower interest (8%–9.5%)

- Tenure up to 30 years

- Tax deductions under Sections 80C and 24(b)

✅ Checklist 29: Before Taking a Home Loan

1. Is the property legally approved?

2. Do I qualify for the PMAY subsidy?

3. Is the EMI affordable long-term?

4. Have I considered legal and processing charges?

13.4 Gold Loans – Fast Funds with Your Assets

"Gold loans are trending. Worth considering?" Aman asked.

"Yes, especially for short-term needs," Ankit said. "They're quick and secure."

Benefits:

- Disbursed within hours

- Lower interest than personal loans (7%–13%)

- No income proof needed

✅ Checklist 30: Using Gold Loans Wisely

1. Know the LTV (Loan-to-Value)—usually 75%

2. Opt for banks/NBFCs with secure vaults

3. Choose repayment style: EMI or bullet

13.5 Education Loans – Investing in Learning

"My cousin wants to study in Canada. Can she get an education loan?" Aman asked.

"Definitely," Ankit said. "Many banks fund both domestic and international courses."

Benefits:

- Moratorium during studies

- Tax deduction under Section 80E

- No collateral up to ₹7.5 lakh

✅ Checklist 31: Before Applying

1. Do banks recognize the course?

2. Can a parent be a co-borrower?

3. Have I calculated the total repayment after the moratorium?

13.6 Vehicle Loans – Drive Your Dream

"What about buying a car?" Aman asked. "Loan or full payment?"

"Loan, if it fits your budget," Ankit said. "Auto loans help preserve liquidity."

Benefits:

- Up to 100% financing

- Fast processing

- Tenure up to 7 years

✅ Checklist 32: Auto Loan Tips

1. Compare ex-showroom vs on-road funding

2. Understand total interest cost

3. Can you handle EMI + running costs?

13.7 Loan Against Property – Big Borrowing for Big Needs

"I've got a small commercial shop. Can I get a loan on that?" Aman asked.

"Absolutely," Ankit replied. "Loan Against Property (LAP) is great for large, long-term needs."

Benefits:

- High loan amounts (based on property value)

- Long tenure (up to 15 years)

- Lower interest rates than unsecured loans

13.8 The Golden Rule – Borrow Smart, Not Just Fast

"Any final advice?" Aman asked.

"Simple," Ankit said. "Borrow only what you need—and what you can repay. Loans can empower you, but mismanaged, they become a burden."

✅ Checklist 33: Golden Rules of Personal Borrowing

1. Keep EMI below 40% of your monthly income

2. Compare at least three lenders

3. Maintain a good credit score (700+)

4. Avoid borrowing for consumption unless necessary

5. Always read the fine print—fees, foreclosure, penalties

In Summary

Aman smiled, "Turns out loans aren't just for crisis—they can fund dreams too."

Ankit nodded, "Exactly. Whether it's a home, education, vehicle, or business need, choosing the right loan makes all the difference."

Aman chuckled, "Now that I've mastered borrowing, I guess it's time to face the legal maze of fundraising."

Ankit replied, "Right on cue—next up, we **untangle the legal and compliance side of raising funds.**"

Chapter 14

Navigating Legal and Compliance in Fundraising

Aman sat in his office, flipping through a pile of documents. "Ankit," he said over the phone, "I thought raising funds was the hard part—but these legal requirements are giving me a headache!"

Ankit chuckled. "Welcome to the world of fundraising compliance. But don't worry—I'll walk you through everything you need to know. Let's make sure you stay on the right side of the law."

14.1 Why Legal Compliance Matters in Fundraising

Aman sighed. "Why do I even need to bother with all these legalities?"

"Because one mistake can cost you—financially and legally," Ankit warned. "Proper compliance protects you, your investors, and your business."

He continued, "Investors trust businesses that follow the rules. Without the right documentation, you could face legal disputes, tax penalties, or even lose your funding."

☑ Checklist 34: Key Legal Considerations Before Raising Funds

1. **Business Structure** – Is your company set up correctly for investment (e.g., Private Limited Company, LLP)?

2. **Investment Agreements** – Are clear, legally binding agreements in place?

3. **Compliance Filings** – Have you filed with MCA, SEBI, or RBI (if applicable)?

4. **Investor Rights** – Are shareholder rights and exit clauses clearly defined?

5. **Tax Implications** – Are you aware of the tax consequences for both you and the investor?

14.2 Choosing the Right Business Structure for Fundraising

"So, does my business structure affect my ability to raise funds?" Aman asked.

"Absolutely," Ankit confirmed. "Investors prefer Private Limited Companies because they offer better governance and exit opportunities."

☑ **Template 20: Business Structures & Funding Suitability**

Business Structure	Ideal For	Suitability for Fundraising
Sole Proprietorship	Small, independent businesses	Limited—Not ideal for equity funding
Partnership Firm	Small teams with shared ownership	Limited—Difficult to raise external funds
Limited Liability Partnership	Service-based firms	Moderate—Good for strategic investors
Private Limited Company	Scalable businesses and startups	High—Preferred for equity investors
Public Limited Company	Large-scale businesses	High—For IPO and large capital raises

"Switching to a Private Limited structure could ease future fundraising," Ankit added.

14.3 Essential Legal Documents for Fundraising

Aman shook his head. "So many documents—what's actually essential?"

Ankit smiled. "Let's focus on the must-haves. Here's your checklist."

☑ **Checklist 35: Must-Have Legal Documents**

1. **Term Sheet** – A non-binding summary of the investment terms.

2. **Shareholders' Agreement** – Defines investor rights and exit options.

3. **Valuation Report** – Certifies your company's value for equity issuance.

4. **Employment Contracts** – Ensures key personnel are locked in.

5. **Cap Table** – Tracks shareholding and equity distribution.

14.4 Understanding Investor Rights and Protections

Aman frowned. "What kind of rights do investors usually ask for?"

"Depends on the type of investor," Ankit said. "But here are the most common ones."

☑ Template 21: Common Investor Rights

Investor Right	Description
Board Seat	Right to appoint a director on your board.
Anti-Dilution	Protection against future lower valuations.
Exit Rights	Right to sell shares during exit events.
Information Rights	Access to regular financial reports.
Drag-Along Rights	Forces minority shareholders to sell in a majority sale.

"Don't just give away these rights—negotiate carefully," Ankit warned.

14.5 Compliance with Regulatory Authorities

Aman scratched his head. "What filings do I need to make once I raise funds?"

"It depends on the type of investment," Ankit explained. "Here's a breakdown."

✅ **Checklist 36: Compliance Filings for Fundraising**

1. **MCA Filings** – This is for issuing new shares and updating the company's structure.

2. **RBI Compliance** – If foreign investors are involved (FEMA regulations).

3. **SEBI Compliance** – If funds are raised through public channels or angel investors,

4. **Income Tax Reporting** – Declare funds raised under the proper sections.

5. **Annual Returns** – Update shareholding patterns in annual filings.

"Failing to file can lead to **penalties and legal action**," Ankit warned.

14.6 Managing Post-Funding Compliance

Aman groaned. "Does compliance ever end?"

"Not if you want to scale," Ankit grinned. "Here's what to track after raising funds."

✅ Checklist 37: Ongoing Compliance After Fundraising

1. **Investor Reporting** – Share quarterly/annual performance reports.

2. **Cap Table Updates** – Keep an accurate record of shareholder changes.

3. **Board Resolutions** – Document major decisions through proper resolutions.

4. **Tax Compliance** – Ensure TDS and GST filings are in order.

5. **ESOP Tracking** – If offering employee equity, maintain updated records.

14.7 Common Legal Pitfalls to Avoid

Aman leaned back. "What mistakes should I watch out for?"

Ankit chuckled. "Glad you asked—many founders trip over there."

✅ Checklist 38: Legal Mistakes to Avoid

1. **Skipping Due Diligence** – Not preparing clear records before raising funds.

2. **Ignoring Contracts** – Relying on verbal agreements instead of written ones.

3. **Over-Dilution** – Giving away too much equity too early.

4. **Incomplete Filings** – Failing to report new investments correctly.

5. **Non-Disclosure Issues** – Sharing confidential data without NDAs.

Aman nodded. "Okay, I'll double-check everything before meeting investors."

"Smart move," Ankit smiled. "Good compliance equals smoother growth."

In Summary

As they wrapped up, Aman felt more confident. "Thanks, Ankit. This feels manageable now."

"It always is—when you know what to do," Ankit grinned. "Stay compliant, and your business can scale without hiccups."

Key Takeaways:

1. **Business Structure Matters** – Choose a structure that supports funding.

2. **Document Everything** – Use proper agreements to protect all parties.

3. **Know the Rules** – Stay informed on legal filings and investor rights.

4. **Stay Compliant** – Post-funding compliance is an ongoing
   responsibility.

Aman smiled. "Let's keep things legal—and keep growing."

Chapter 15

Scaling with Smart Funding – Your Roadmap Forward

Aman and Ankit sat in a café, the buzz of entrepreneurs around them. Aman stirred his coffee, thoughtfully expressing, "We've covered so much—from understanding funding types to managing compliance. But now, how do I actually scale up without losing focus?"

Ankit smiled. "That's the real challenge—scaling sustainably. Funding is a tool, not the end goal. Let's break down a practical roadmap to help you scale smartly while staying financially strong."

15.1 Building a Scalable Business Model

Aman leaned in. "So, what's the first step?"

"Everything starts with your business model," Ankit explained. "You need a model that can grow without breaking under pressure."

"Think about it—can your operations handle a 5x growth without chaos?"

✅ **Checklist 39: Designing a Scalable Business Model**

1. **Revenue Streams** – Are your income sources diversified and repeatable?

2. **Operational Efficiency** – Can your systems handle increased demand?

3. **Customer Retention** – Are you building a loyal customer base?

4. **Automation** – What processes can be automated to save time?

5. **Talent Strategy** – Are you hiring and training for future needs?

Aman nodded. "So, I need to ensure my systems and people can grow with the business."

"Exactly," Ankit agreed. "A shaky foundation won't support rapid growth."

15.2 Allocating Funds for Maximum Growth

Aman asked, "Once I raise funds, where should I invest first?"

Ankit replied, "Prioritize areas that directly drive growth and efficiency."

✅ **Checklist 40: Smart Fund Allocation Strategy**

1. **Core Operations** – Strengthen your production or service delivery.

2. **Technology** – Invest in scalable tech to streamline workflows.

3. **Marketing & Sales** – Focus on customer acquisition and brand building.

4. **Talent Acquisition** – Hire specialized talent to drive growth.

5. **Reserves** – Keep a portion for emergencies and new opportunities.

"Balance is key—don't burn through your capital," Ankit warned. "Always measure ROI."

15.3 Measuring Growth Metrics That Matter

"What metrics should I track to know I'm scaling the right way?" Aman asked.

"Investors love data-backed decisions," Ankit said. "Focus on key performance indicators (KPIs) that show real progress."

✅ **Template 22: Essential Growth Metrics Dashboard**

Metric	Why It Matters
Customer Acquisition Cost (CAC)	Measures the cost of acquiring a new customer.
Lifetime Value (LTV)	Predicts long-term revenue per customer.
Gross Margin	Ensures profitability as you scale.
Burn Rate	Tracks monthly cash outflow.

Churn Rate	Monitors customer retention.
Runway	Shows how many months of cash you have.

"Track these metrics monthly," Ankit advised. "They tell the real growth story."

15.4 Leveraging Strategic Partnerships for Faster Growth

"Can partnerships help me scale faster?" Aman asked.

"Absolutely," Ankit said. "Strategic collaborations give you access to new markets and resources without heavy costs."

☑ Checklist 41: Building Strategic Partnerships

1. **Complementary Services** – Partner with businesses offering complementary products.

2. **Distribution Channels** – Collaborate for wider market reach.

3. **Technology Integration** – Use tech partnerships to enhance your offering.

4. **Co-Marketing** – Share marketing efforts for greater visibility.

5. **Government Schemes** – Leverage public-private partnerships for incentives.

"Good partnerships amplify your growth—without draining your resources," Ankit noted.

15.5 Preparing for Future Funding Rounds

Aman grinned. "So, when do I plan my next funding round?"

Ankit laughed. "Once you show traction and clear milestones, it's time to level up again."

✅ Checklist 42: Preparing for the Next Funding Round

1. **Proven Business Model** – Demonstrate a scalable, profitable model.

2. **Financial Discipline** – Maintain clean books and regular audits.

3. **Investor Communication** – Keep existing investors updated.

4. **Clear Use of Funds** – Define how new capital will accelerate growth.

5. **Legal Readiness** – Ensure compliance with previous investment agreements.

"Always raise with a purpose," Ankit said. "Investors back businesses that know their next move."

15.6 Avoiding Common Scaling Pitfalls

"What mistakes should I avoid when scaling?" Aman asked.

Ankit leaned back. "Here are the most common ones—and how to dodge them."

☑ **Checklist 43: Scaling Mistakes to Avoid**

1. **Over-Hiring** – Expand your team too fast, and you'll burn cash.

2. **Uncontrolled Spending** – Stay disciplined—don't overspend on non-essentials.

3. **Neglecting Culture** – Protect your company culture as you grow.

4. **Ignoring Customer Feedback** – Keep adapting based on customer needs.

5. **Poor Cash Flow Management** – Always track and optimize your burn rate.

"Scaling is a marathon, not a sprint," Ankit said. "Pace yourself."

15.7 Your Smart Funding Roadmap – Putting It All Together

Aman smiled. "This has been a game-changer. But how do I keep everything on track?"

Ankit pulled out a neatly organized roadmap. "Here's your action plan. Follow these steps, and you'll stay on course."

☑ Template 23: Your Smart Funding & Scaling Roadmap

Stage	Key Focus Areas	Action Items
Seed Stage	Idea Validation & Market Fit	Build MVP, Secure Early Funding
Early-Stage Growth	Operations & Customer Acquisition	Optimize Processes, Track Key Metrics
Scale-Up Phase	Expanding Market Reach	Strengthen Partnerships, Prepare Next Round
Growth Stage	Long-Term Sustainability	Focus on Profitability, Diversify Revenue

Aman shook Ankit's hand. "Thanks for everything—I'm ready to scale!"

Ankit smiled. "You've got this, Aman. With smart funding and clear execution, the sky's the limit."

In Summary

1. **Think Big, Plan Smart** – Scale with a sustainable business model.

2. **Track Metrics That Matter** – Data drives better funding decisions.

3. **Use Funds Wisely** – Prioritize growth without waste.

4. **Prepare for the Next Step** – Each funding round sets the stage for the next.

As Aman walked out, he felt empowered—his journey from startup to scale-up had just begun.

Chapter 16

The Mentor's Legacy – How Guidance Shapes Growth

Aman stood on the balcony of his newly expanded office, overlooking the bustling city. It had been two years since he first sat with Ankit, confused and overwhelmed by the world of funding. Today, his company has grown from a small startup to a thriving business with multiple funding rounds, a strong customer base, and a clear roadmap for the future.

As he sipped his coffee, his phone buzzed. It was Ankit.

"Congratulations on closing your Series A funding!" Ankit's voice was warm with pride.

Aman smiled. "I couldn't have done it without you, Ankit. You've been more than just a funding advisor—you've been my guide through every twist and turn."

16.1 The Beginning – More Than Just an Advisor

Aman's mind drifted back to their first meeting. He had approached Ankit, unsure if his business idea could ever attract serious investment.

"You didn't just explain funding," Aman said. "You gave me confidence. You helped me see how I could turn a small idea into a scalable business."

Ankit chuckled. "Well, you had the vision. My job was to provide the roadmap and keep you from falling into the common traps."

✅ Checklist 44: What to Look for in a Funding Mentor

1. **Experience Across Funding Types** – Understands the nuances of debt and equity financing.

2. **Strategic Thinking** – Helps align funding decisions with long-term business goals.

3. **Compliance Expertise** – Ensures legal and regulatory adherence.

4. **Network & Relationships** – Connects you with investors, legal experts, and financial partners.

5. **Personal Commitment** – Genuinely invested in your growth beyond transactions.

16.2 The Power of Strategic Guidance

"You didn't just help me raise funds—you showed me how to use them wisely," Aman reflected.

Ankit nodded. "Many founders think raising capital is the finish line. But really, it's just the beginning. My role was to help you allocate funds effectively, track metrics, and prepare for every next step."

✅ Template 24: The Mentor's Role in a Founder's Journey

Stage	Mentor's Role
Idea Stage	Validate the business model and identify funding needs.
Seed Funding	Prepare investor pitches and structure the deal.
Scaling Up	Optimize fund utilization and monitor growth metrics.
Compliance & Governance	Ensure regulatory compliance and protect legal interests.
Future Rounds	Identify new funding opportunities and guide negotiations.

16.3 Navigating Challenges Together

Aman recalled a moment when things almost fell apart. "During our first debt raise, when that investor hesitated, I thought everything would collapse."

"I remember," Ankit said. "But we had a backup plan. That's the value of thinking ahead. Having a contingency strategy saved you."

✅ Checklist 45: How a Mentor Supports You Through Challenges

1. **Crisis Management** – Provides alternative strategies during setbacks.

2. **Investor Negotiation** – Helps navigate tough conversations and deal terms.

3. **Operational Insights** – Guides efficient cash flow and fund utilization.

4. **Emotional Support** – Offers perspective when decisions get overwhelming.

5. **Future Vision** – Keeps you focused on the long-term picture.

16.4 From Advisor to Partner in Growth

Over time, Ankit became more than a consultant—he was a trusted partner.

"You didn't just give advice—you celebrated the wins and stood by me during the struggles," Aman said, his voice filled with gratitude.

"That's what a true advisor does," Ankit replied. "Your success is my success."

✅ Checklist 46: The Mentor-Entrepreneur Partnership

1. **Trust & Transparency** – Open communication at every stage.

2. **Mutual Growth** – Aligning personal and business growth goals.

3. **Long-Term Vision** – Thinking beyond immediate funding needs.

4. **Continuous Learning** – Sharing new insights and strategies.

5. **Legacy Building** – Working together to create a lasting impact.

16.5 Paying It Forward – Becoming a Mentor

Aman leaned against the railing. "You've given me so much knowledge. I want to pass that on to other entrepreneurs."

Ankit smiled. "And that's how the ecosystem grows. Your journey can inspire others who stand where you once did."

✅ **Checklist 47: How to Become a Mentor for Future Entrepreneurs**

1. **Share Your Journey** – Be open about your struggles and lessons.

2. **Offer Practical Guidance** – Provide actionable, real-world advice.

3. **Be Accessible** – Make time to guide and support others.

4. **Encourage Resilience** – Help mentees navigate failure and bounce back.

5. **Foster Collaboration** – Connect entrepreneurs to resources and networks.

In Summary – The Power of a Strong Mentor

Aman: "Thank you, Ankit. I wouldn't be here without your guidance. You've been more than a mentor—you've been like a partner in this journey."

Ankit: "You've done the work, Aman. I just helped you see the path. A mentor's role is to guide, support, and help you avoid pitfalls. The real power of mentorship is in helping you unlock your potential and build confidence for the road ahead."

Aman: "I'm ready for whatever comes next. And I hope to pay it forward, just like you did for me."

Ankit: "That's the spirit. Keep inspiring others, and remember, this is just the beginning."

As Aman stood looking out over the city, he realized that with Ankit's mentorship, he wasn't just building a company—he was building a legacy. The power of a mentor lies in their ability to transform uncertainty into confidence and to guide you through the toughest moments. With that kind of support, the sky was truly the limit.

THE END – BUT YOUR JOURNEY IS JUST BEGINNING!

Ready to scale with the right funding? Let's Make It Happen.

Scaling your business is one of the most exciting—and challenging—phases of growth. With the right strategy, resources, and support, you can unlock new opportunities, expand your operations, and achieve long-term success. Just like Aman did with my guidance, you can scale your business sustainably and confidently. But it all starts with the right approach.

As someone who has helped businesses across India navigate funding, operations, and growth challenges, I understand the pitfalls and the path to success.

Option 1: Struggling to Scale Without Support?

Scaling a business isn't something you should tackle alone. Many entrepreneurs try to do everything themselves, but without expert advice and strategic planning, it's easy to face unnecessary setbacks. You might find yourself burning through capital without seeing growth, losing sight of key metrics, or even missing out on funding opportunities. I've seen too many businesses fail because they didn't have the right mentorship or support at crucial stages. Don't risk that for your business. Let's address these challenges before they become roadblocks.

Option 2: Book a Consultation with Me

I've spent the last 10 years helping more than 100 entrepreneurs to raise funding, optimize their operations, and scale their businesses effectively. With my experience and deep understanding of the funding landscape, I'll guide you in building a scalable business model, ensuring that you don't just grow—but grow smartly and sustainably. Let's discuss your challenges, plan your next steps, and get you on the road to achieving your business goals.

Your Journey to Growth Begins Now

Whether you're ready to jumpstart your scaling journey with expert guidance or you're struggling to get past a growth hurdle, I'm here to help. Let's work together to navigate the complexities of scaling your business, secure the right funding, and set you up for sustainable success. For more details Email us on cakrishnabaheti@gmail.com or scan below

★ ★ ★ ★

May I Ask You For a Small Favor?

First, I want to thank you for reading this book. You could have chosen any other book, but you took mine, and I appreciate this. I hope you have at least a few actionable insights that will positively impact your daily life.

Can I ask for 30 seconds more of your time?

I'd love it if you could leave a review of the book. That will help me grow my readership by encouraging folks to take a chance on my books.

Keeping it straight - **reviews are the lifeblood of any author.**

It will take less than a minute of your time but will tremendously help me reach out to more people.

If you liked this book, **please consider posting an honest review on your preferred retailer. And I'd love to see your review.**

Thanks for your support!